Foods of the Caribbean

Barbara Sheen

KIDHAVEN PRESS
An imprint of Thomson Gale, a part of The Thomson Corporation

Detroit • New York • San Francisco • New Haven, Conn. • Waterville, Maine • London

For more information, contact
KidHaven Press
27500 Drake Rd.
Farmington Hills, MI 48331-3535
Or you can visit our Internet site at http://www.gale.com

LIBRARY OF CONGRESS CATALOGING-IN-PUBLICATION DATA

Sheen, Barbara.
  Foods of the Caribbean / by Barbara Sheen.
    p. cm. — (A taste of culture)
  Includes bibliographical references and index.
  ISBN 978-0-7377-3774-5 (hardcover)
  1. Cookery, Caribbean—Juvenile literature. I. Title.
  TX716.A1S5 2007
  641.59729—dc22
 	
                                                              2007021867

ISBN-10: 0-7377-3774-3

Printed in the United States of America

Contents

Chapter 1
Exciting and Colorful   4

Chapter 2
A Bite of History   20

Chapter 3
Life Tastes Good   33

Chapter 4
A Warm Welcome   43

Metric Conversions   55

Notes   56

Glossary   58

For Further Exploration   60

Index   62

Picture Credits   64

About the Author   64

Exciting and Colorful

The Caribbean is the name given to the 30 large and more than 1,000 small islands that dot the Caribbean Sea. Stretching more than 1,800 miles from Cuba in the north to Trinidad in the south, these islands reach from the tip of Florida to the coast of South America. They include the nations of Jamaica, Cuba, the Bahamas, Puerto Rico, Haiti, the Dominican Republic, and Aruba, among others.

A tropical climate, rich soil, and waters teeming with life make food plentiful throughout the islands. Caribbean chefs have many foods to choose from. Meat, vegetables, beans, and rice are important parts of the Caribbean diet. But it is fish and seafood, tropical fruits, and herbs and spices that give Caribbean cooking

FLORIDA (U.S.)

ATLANTIC OCEAN

CUBA

HAITI

DOMINICAN REPUBLIC

Fish	
Nuts	
Coconuts	
Fruit	
Pepper	
Chicken	
Pork	
Beans	
Rice and peas	
Tea	

CARIBBEAN SEA

FOOD REGIONS OF THE CARIBBEAN

SOUTH AMERICA

its unique flavor. They make Caribbean cooking as fragrant and colorful as the islands themselves.

Fish and Seafood

The Caribbean Sea and the many waterways that cross the islands are home to a wide variety of water creatures. Fish and seafood have been a vital part of Caribbean people's diet ever since the islands' earliest inhabitants, the **Arawak** and **Carib** Indians, caught fish on the ends of their spears in the islands' shallow

The Caribbean is dotted with islands surrounded by the impossibly blue sea, which contains the main staple of the islanders' diet—seafood.

Not only does the conch have a beautiful shell, its meat is also a delicious meal that is prepared in many ways.

coastal waters more than 1,000 years ago. Even today, fishing is a common island pastime. According to chefs Jinx and Jefferson Morgan, "Dipping a net into the water just outside one's doorstep is often the first step toward dinner in the Caribbean."[1]

Red snapper, swordfish, shark, flying fish, conch, crab, lobster, and shrimp are just a few of the many water creatures found here. These are cooked in a variety of ways. They may be dipped in cornmeal and fried, boiled in orange sauce, wrapped in banana leaves

Flying Fish

Flying fish are interesting creatures. These fish do not actually fly. They glide through the air. To get into the air, they swim at speeds of up to 30 miles per hour (48 kmph) to the water's surface then jump out of the water. Once in the air, they spread their large fins like wings. To an observer, it looks like the fish are flying.

The fish are found throughout the Caribbean and especially in the waters around Barbados. Steamed flying fish with coo-coo, a cornmeal mush, is the national dish of Barbados. Flying fish are so important in Barbados that they are featured in the country's national symbol.

and baked, or grilled over an open fire and topped with hot sauce, lime juice, or mango salsa. Or they may be **marinated** in a mixture of lime juice, onions, garlic, and hot peppers, then **poached** to make a dish called **blaff**. It is a dish named for the sound the fish makes when it is dropped into the hot poaching liquid.

Fish and seafood are also **sautéed** (saw-tayd) with onions, garlic, chile peppers, tomatoes, and spices. **Conch** (konk), the sea creature that lives inside a large spiral seashell, is often prepared in this manner. Because conch can be rubbery, Caribbean cooks beat the meat with a mallet to tenderize it before frying it. Conch is also used in salads, made into burgers, or rubbed with hot peppers and lime juice and eaten raw. According to author Bruce Geddes, "You'll be hard pressed to find a place that doesn't serve it."[2]

Hot and Spicy Nuts

Islanders add spice to almost everything, including the cashew nuts that grow in the islands. For this recipe, you can substitute peanuts for cashews and add more or less spice depending on your taste.

Ingredients
2 cups cashew nuts
¼ cup butter
1 teaspoon chili powder
1 teaspoon salt

Instructions
1. Melt the butter in a frying pan over low heat. Add the nuts and cook for five minutes.
2. Drain the nuts. Put them in a bowl and sprinkle with the chili powder and salt. Toss well.

Makes 2 cups of spiced nuts.

Hot and spicy cashews are a popular snack.

Freshly Caught

No matter the type of fish or seafood, or the way it is prepared, one thing is certain—it must be freshly caught. The idea of eating day-old or frozen fish is unthinkable for islanders. Fishermen sell their catch right on the beaches or carry them in buckets through the streets. Waiting cooks transfer the fish right into their cooking pots. Chef John De Mers describes a typical scene in the U.S. Virgin Islands: "Women with woven baskets waited on the sand as the men pulled up their boats and started displaying their rainbow wares. Once the haggling on the beach was done, the men pitched their… fish into wooden carts and pushed them through the streets and towns calling out each type…. Women in brightly colored bandanas flung open their shutters and placed orders."[3]

A Tropical Bounty

A variety of trees loaded with fragrant and juicy tropical fruits grow wild throughout the islands. "The beaches,

The mortar and pestle are used to mash plantains to make mofongo.

Outdoor markets sell the area's bountiful fruits, vegetables, spices, and seafood.

the valleys, even the mountainsides are crazy with this bounty—bursting open, ripening, taking on color in the warm, moist air,"[4] says De Mers.

Islanders use fruit in everything—from salads, desserts, snacks, and juices to garnishes for meat and fish. Some of the fruits, such as bananas, oranges, grapefruit, watermelon, and pineapple are well known in North America. Others are less familiar.

Among the less familiar ones are orange-fleshed papayas (pa-pie-uhs). Blended with milk, papayas make sweet and delicious smoothies. Unripe papayas are cooked and eaten like vegetables, as are green

Although ackee is a fruit, it tastes like scrambled eggs when it is prepared.

Coconuts

Coconuts grow wild on tall palm trees throughout the islands. The white nutmeat is used in many Caribbean dishes. Shrimp are often rolled in shredded coconut before cooking. Coconut cookies, chips, breads, cakes, ice cream, and puddings are all popular here. Coconut water or juice, which is found inside the center of the nut, makes a refreshing island drink. To get to it, islanders chop off the top of the coconut and insert a straw. Some cooks substitute coconut juice for water when they are cooking rice or beans.

Coconut milk is also used in Caribbean cooking. It is not actually milk. It is made from mashed coconut meat. Seafood, fish, rice, and vegetables are often cooked in it.

Both the meat and the juice of the coconut are used throughout the islands.

mangos. **Plantains**, too, take the place of vegetables. Although they look like large, green bananas, they are fried like potatoes or boiled, mashed, and mixed with meat to make mofongo, a popular dish in Puerto Rico.

Ackee is another popular fruit that islanders use in their cooking. On the outside it has reddish skin. Inside are yellow pods. The pods are poisonous until the fruit splits open. This means it is ripe. Once the fruit is ripe, islanders fry the pods, which look and taste a lot like scrambled eggs, and serve them with fish.

Fruits are also made into "sky juice," the syrup that flavors snow cones. Or, they are transformed into jellies, jams, and sweet and savory relishes. Mangos, for example, are used in relishes, salsas, and spicy sauces. **Guavas** (gwa-vahs), sweet pear-shaped fruits, are used in jellies and to make a sticky paste that is called guava cheese. Since more than 100 different varieties of guavas grow in the Caribbean, the fruit is extremely popular.

Herbs and Spices

Herbs and spices are almost as abundant as fruits in the Caribbean. Islanders love flavoring their foods with relishes and sauces made with zesty spices. Before refrigerators existed, rubbing or bathing foods in spices helped preserve them in the tropical heat. That is one reason it was a favorite practice of the Arawak Indians.

Many different kinds of herbs and spices grow in the Caribbean. They are so plentiful that the island

Fruit Salad

Islanders eat fruit salad for breakfast, snacks, and desserts. Any fresh fruits can be used.

Ingredients

1 small, fresh pineapple, peeled and cut into cubes, or one 8 oz.-can pineapple chunks, drained
1 mango, peeled and cut into cubes
1 banana, sliced
2 oranges, peeled, seeded, and sectioned
1/3 cup flaked coconut
1 tablespoon honey

Instructions

1. Combine all the fruit in a large bowl and mix.
2. Drizzle the honey on top. Sprinkle with coconut.

Serves 4. For a special treat, serve the fruit salad with vanilla yogurt or ice cream.

Fruit salad can be made with any fresh, ripe fruit.

Allspice, called pimento, is one of many spices that grow in the Caribbean.

of Grenada is nicknamed "The Spice Island." Indeed, many of the herbs and spices used in North America and Europe come from the Caribbean.

Allspice, which is called **pimento** (pee-men-toe) in the islands, is probably the most popular spice in the Caribbean. It tastes like a mix of nutmeg and pepper, two other spices that grow in the islands. Allspice is used to flavor stews, meats, and seafood.

Fresh cinnamon is also popular. The sticks are sold in little bundles and used to flavor drinks, porridges, and desserts. Thyme is another favorite. It is added to spicy sauces. But the main ingredients in Caribbean sauces, pastes, and rubs are hot chili peppers.

Although most Caribbean cooks make their own hot sauces, a wide variety can be found at outdoor markets.

Hot Peppers

Islanders grow a wide variety of fiery peppers. The Scotch bonnet, a popular favorite, is fifty times hotter than a jalapeño pepper. It has a crinkled top that looks like a little cap, or bonnet, and an intense taste. Islanders mix it with an assortment of spices to create an array of hot sauces. These sauces are found on every kitchen table. They are used much like catsup is in the United States. They are so important to Caribbean meals that chef Steven Raichlen reports that a friend of his from the Bahamas "would never leave his home without a flask of this fiery condiment in his pocket."[5]

Almost every Caribbean cook has his or her own special hot sauce recipe. The sauces can be scorching or mild. They can contain sour or sweet

The Scotch bonnet is a favorite pepper that is used to fire up many Caribbean dishes.

fruits. They can be red, orange, green, or yellow. The taste depends on the different spices they contain. Says Raichlen: "There are few places in the world where you find such a diverse assortment of seasonings and condiments."[6]

Or, for that matter, so many other foods—clearly the Caribbean islands are blessed with an abundant food supply. Fresh seafood and fish, juicy fruits, and fiery spices are among everyone's favorites. These ingredients reflect the warmth, vivid colors, and sweet scents of the islands.

A Bite of History

Favorite dishes vary from island to island. No matter the island or the dish, Caribbean cooking reflects the area's rich history and the different groups of people who have made the islands their home.

Spicy Barbeque

The warm climate of the Caribbean causes meat to spoil easily. The Arawak Indians solved this problem in a clever way. They rubbed meat with a blend of lime juice and spices. The combination added flavor to the meat and, because the spices have antibacterial properties, helped to preserve it. As a result, if they had a large quantity of meat, they did not have to cook it all at once.

India's Contribution

Many people from India came to live in the Caribbean in the 19th century. They worked as indentured servants, unpaid workers who contracted to work for a set number of years in exchange for their passage to the Caribbean and their room and board.

They influenced cooking throughout the islands, especially in Trinidad. Trinidadian cooks borrowed many recipes from them, including curry. Curry dishes feature meat, seafood, vegetables, and poultry cooked in a spicy sauce. Trinidadians even cook bananas in curry sauce and season cashew nuts with curry spices.

Roti, another Indian specialty, is also popular. It is fried bread stuffed with different curries. Shops selling roti can be found all over Trinidad.

Boucan (boo-can), the Arawak cooking method, was also interesting. It involved placing the meat over a fire pit filled with fragrant green allspice wood. As it burned, the fragrant wood gave the meat a sweet and smoky scent and flavor. Centuries later, pirates who roamed the Caribbean Sea adopted the cooking method. In fact, pirates are often called "buccaneers," a named derived from this cooking style.

In the 18th century, a group of escaped slaves on the island of Jamaica used this same cooking style to keep themselves alive. The group, who were known as the **Maroons**, rebelled against the slave owners and hid in the island's Blue Mountains. They killed wild boars for

The combination of seasonings to make jerk is unique to each cook.

food and marinated the meat in a mixture of allspice, chilis, black pepper, garlic, lime juice, cinnamon, and nutmeg. The mixture not only kept the meat from spoiling, it tenderized it and gave it a zesty flavor. The longer the meat marinated, the softer and more flavorful it became, which is why they often marinated it for 24 hours. The Maroons cooked the meat on a network of allspice branches. By the time it was done, the meat was so tender that it could be pulled or jerked right off the bone, which is how the dish got its name—**jerk pork**.

Modern jerk dishes use the meat from domestic pigs or chickens, which also have a place in island history. These animals are not native to the Caribbean. The

European settlers who colonized the different islands in the 16th century brought the animals to the islands.

Today, jerk pork and jerk chicken are popular throughout the Caribbean. In Jamaica, jerk huts, where fresh jerk is cooked and sold, dot the countryside. Blue smoke and a mouth-watering aroma make the huts easy to find. They are always crowded with hungry islanders and tourists.

Almost everyone has a favorite jerk hut. And every cook has his or her own special jerk spice blend. The end result, according to chef Dorinda Hafner, "is so delicious that the anticipation of eating it is enough

Jerk chicken, along with jerk pork, is a very popular dish in the islands.

Jerk Chicken

Jerk chicken is not hard to make. The longer the chicken marinates the tastier it is. You can cook the chicken on a grill or in an oven or broiler. Jamaican jerk sauce can be used instead of home-made marinade. It is sold in most supermarkets.

Ingredients

4 chicken breasts
1 jalapeño pepper, seeded and minced
2 green onions, minced
¼ cup each of lime juice, orange juice, soy sauce
1 garlic clove, minced
1 teaspoon each of allspice, thyme, cinnamon, sugar, olive oil

Instructions

1. To make the marinade, combine all ingredients except the chicken in a large bowl and mix well.
2. Pour the marinade into a large resealable bag and add the chicken. Make sure the chicken is covered with the marinade, then put in the refrigerator overnight.
3. Line a broiler pan with nonstick foil, or spray it with cooking spray. Put the chicken in the pan and spoon on the marinade. Turn the oven to Broil.
4. Add more marinade as the chicken broils. The chicken is done when it is no longer pink inside, about 10–15 minutes.

Serves 4.

Jerk chicken is popular all over the islands.

to make me click my fingers and shake my head with excitement."[7]

One-Pot Delicacies

The African slaves also played an important part in creating another popular island cooking style, the one-pot meal. The slaves were given the poorest cuts of meat and just one cooking pot. It was a large, black cauldron called a **canaree**. Using the pot to slow-cook tough meat along with spices, liquid, and vegetables flavored and tenderized the meat. Although the resulting creations were originally meant for the slaves alone, the smells coming from the canaree were so tantalizing that soon both slaves and slave owners were eating these dishes.

The many soups and stews that are island favorites

Caribbean Jerk Dishes and North American Jerky

It is easy to confuse Caribbean jerk dishes with jerky, a popular North American snack. But they are not the same. Jerky is dried meat. To make it, strips of meat are salted and spiced and then dried in the sun or in an oven. This removes all the moisture from the meat and keeps it from spoiling.

Caribbean jerk dishes, on the other hand, use fresh meat. Caribbean jerk is similar to jerky in one way. It is also spiced, and, in the past, one job of the spices was to keep the meat from spoiling.

arose from these one-pot recipes. Among them is **pepperpot**, as it is called in much of the southern Caribbean. It is also known as sopa de quingombo (soh-pah day keen-gohm-bo) in Puerto Rico and **callaloo** in Jamaica. Callaloo is also the name for a leafy green vegetable similar to spinach that gives the dish its green color.

Depending on the cook and the island, pepperpot may be thick like a stew or thin and velvety like a soup. It features **cassareep** (kas-a-reep), a substance made from the juice of the **cassava** (kas-sah-vuh), a starchy root vegetable. Interestingly, cassava contains a poison. But the Arawak Indians developed a way to boil

Callaloo is the leafy green vegetable that is the main ingredient of pepperpot.

Ropa Vieja

Ropa vieja, which means *old clothing* or *rags* in Spanish, is a delicious one-pot meal popular in Cuba. This recipe uses cooked chicken, but cooked turkey, pork, or beef can be substituted.

Ingredients
1 pound cooked chicken, shredded
1 small onion, chopped
1 large tomato, chopped
1 green bell pepper, chopped
1 garlic clove, chopped
2 tablespoons olive oil
salt and pepper to taste

Instructions
1. Heat the oil in a large pan over medium heat. Add the onion, garlic, tomato, and pepper and cook until the onion is lightly browned.
2. Add the meat. Cook on low heat for 5 minutes, stirring often.

Serve over rice. Serves 4.

The foods of the islands were influenced by the different groups of people who settled there.

the vegetable down, which removed the toxin. The African slaves added sugar and spices to the boiled-down syrup and used it as a base for pepperpot. The dish typically contains a variety of ingredients such as callaloo, kale, okra, pork, fish, chilis, onions, and chicken broth. It may also contain beef, yams, squash, carrots, crabmeat, and coconut milk. Some recipes have more than twenty different ingredients, while others are simpler.

Traditionally, after all of the meat is eaten, some of the cooking liquid is kept. It is used to start a new batch of pepperpot. In fact, in the past, on the sugar plantations of Grenada, cauldrons of pepperpot were never removed from the fire. Instead, meat was continually added.

That way, when guests arrived there was always hot pepperpot to greet them. According to chef Norman Van Aken, "On some plantations, they boasted of keeping their pepperpots going for more than twenty years at a stretch."[8]

Rice and Peas

In the Caribbean, beans are often called peas, and rice and peas is a favorite dish throughout the islands. Three of the groups that shaped the history of the area had an important role in making rice and peas popular.

Many different kinds of beans grow in the islands, and each nation has its favorite.

Although the combination of rice and peas may differ from one country to another, most people in the islands eat the dish at least once a day.

The first group, the Spanish, who settled on a number of islands, including Puerto Rico and Cuba, brought rice to the area. The grain was not native to the Caribbean, but it grew well in the rich soil. Even though rice adapted well, the grain did not become a favorite in the Caribbean until the 1830s. At that time, slavery in the islands had ended, and people from Asia came to the Caribbean to work on the sugar plantations. These newcomers brought their love of rice with them. Because of their influence, rice became popular.

Beans, too, have a place in Caribbean history. Some varieties are native to the islands. Although the Indians and early European settlers ate them, it was the African slaves who made them popular. They brought many new types with them, such as black-eyed peas and small yellow pigeon peas.

Over time, Caribbean cooks developed a number of ways to combine rice and beans to create a variety of dishes popular throughout the islands. For instance, "Moors and Christians," the Cuban version of rice and beans, contains black beans and rice spiced with onions, green peppers, tomatoes, pork, cumin (a spice), and black pepper. If red beans are used, Cubans call the dish **congri** (kon-gree). In Martinique and Guadeloupe, black-eyed peas are favored, while in Haiti, lima beans are used. These are cooked with mushrooms. The combination is scooped over fluffy rice to form a dish known as djon djon (de-jon de-jon).

In the Virgin Islands, pigeon peas are popular. There, peas and rice are often topped with fried plantains or a fried egg. Bahamian and Jamaican cooks choose kidney beans. Jamaicans soak the beans in coconut milk, then cook them with cloves, onion, garlic, and thyme. This dish is so popular that Jamaicans jokingly say the dish should be featured on their nation's coat of arms.

But no matter the name of the dish or the combination of ingredients, most people in the Caribbean eat rice and peas at least once a day. It can accompany seafood, meat, or poultry, or it can serve as a meal by itself. De Mers explains that whatever form the dish takes, rice and peas are "a true Caribbean standard."[9]

Whether it is rice and peas in its many forms, jerk pork and chicken, or delectable one-pot creations, the many cultures living on the islands contributed something to the cuisine and made it uniquely Caribbean. The area's rich history has created a wonderful variety of delicious dishes.

Life Tastes Good

"'Life tastes good' proclaims a sign above a roadside food stand in Trinidad."[10]

On the islands, street and roadside food stands, sweet shops, and traveling vendors are almost everywhere. Snacking is a way of life. Vendors tempt islanders with a wide array of savory and sweet choices, including fried delicacies, seafood, and sweet treats.

Crisp and Crunchy

Fried snacks are popular throughout the Caribbean. Some are spicy, while others are salty. But no matter the seasoning, they are all crisp and crunchy. Plantain chips, **chicharrones** (chee-char-roh-nays), and **fritters** are among the most popular.

Plantain chips are the Caribbean answer to potato chips. To make them, the hard green bananalike fruits are peeled and sliced into thin rounds, then deep-fried in hot oil. When the chips are hot and golden, they are put in a paper bag with a sprinkle of salt. The cook shakes the bag. This allows some of the oil to be blotted up by the paper while lightly salting the chips. The results are hot, crisp, and yummy; "perfect," according to chef Jessica B. Harris, "for nibbling."[11]

Chicharrones are similar to chips. They are made by deep-frying pork rinds, strips of pork fat and skin, in oil or lard. The crunchy strips, which are sprinkled with salt, are especially popular in Puerto Rico. Vendors throughout the island fry the crackling treats right in front of waiting customers. Harris describes a typical scene: "You see small stands with large curly, crispy lengths of fried pork rind. The pork rind is weighed out and wrapped in brown paper, which immediately becomes greasy; it is up to you to break the skin down into small bite-sized pieces."[12]

Fritters are another popular fried snack. They are

small cakes or patties made by frying batter in hot oil. Different types of fritters are made with different ingredients. For instance, papaya fritters combine flour and eggs with unripe papayas, while bammy, a popular fritter that is sold all over the islands, is made from grated cassava and salt. Vegetable fritters are also quite popular. These may be made with pumpkin, sweet potatoes, okra, or a mixture of beans and dasheen, the leaves of the taro plant.

Seafood Snacks

Some fritters feature fish or other seafood. Conch fritters and spicy fish fritters called "stamp and go" are good examples. No one knows how stamp and go got its unusual name. The fact that the fritters are

Stamp and go is a unique name for a delicious snack.

sold at bus stops may have helped name them. It is common for passengers to buy a bus ticket, in the form of a stamp, and a bagful of the crunchy fritters to munch on the bus—hence the name stamp and go.

Stamp and go is made with saltfish. Saltfish is the only nonfresh fish that islanders eat. It was first brought to the Caribbean as part of the slave trade. Because the fish is dried and then preserved in salt, it does not spoil easily. This made it a good food to feed the slaves on the long voyage from Africa. And because it was cheap, once the captives reached the islands, saltfish remained a part of their diet.

Over time, saltfish became popular throughout the islands. In stamp and go, the saltfish—usually cod—is soaked in water. This removes the salt, and plumps up and softens the fish, giving it more the taste of fresh fish. Next, the fish is shredded and mixed with chilis, flour, eggs, and onions. The fritters, which look like crab cakes, are fried until they are golden and served with a creamy lime sauce for dipping.

Other versions of fried fish, such as one called "shark and bake" are sold throughout the islands. To make shark and bake, cooks marinate shark meat in a mixture of lime juice and hot sauce. Then they bread the fish and deep-fry it. The lightly browned fish is served wrapped in round, fried bread called bakes and topped with more hot sauce.

Although fried treats are an important part of islanders' diets, it was the European settlers who intro-duced the cooking style to the area. Today, says Van

Aken, "the plazas and streets…are filled with tantalizing aromas—most of which are the products of expert frying."[13]

And for those snackers who prefer a healthier cooking method, there are chilled and spiced seafood salads or grilled fresh fish. Cooks prepare the fish over little grills placed on roadsides, sidewalks, and beaches. Each offers passersby a host of delicious tastes and smells.

Sweet Treats

Since sugar is an important Caribbean crop, it is not surprising that sweet snacks are also popular. On the French- and Spanish-influenced islands, islanders enjoy sweets any time of day. On the British-influenced islands, the British tradition of afternoon tea is followed.

French Sweets

The French islands, which include Martinique, Haiti, and Guadeloupe, have many sweet shops. They showcase candies and pastries behind sparkling glass cases. Most of these delicacies have their origin in France but feature tropical flavors.

Glacés (glah-says) are candied fruits. In France, these are likely to be berries or pears. On the islands, papayas and pineapples are featured. And, like the French, islanders like to dip strawberries in chocolate. Islanders also dip chunks of starfruit, pineapple, and mangos in chocolate.

Even though some islanders prefer coffee to tea, the accompaniment is almost always a sweet treat.

Most of these treats feature tropical fruits or coconuts. Banana coconut bread or orange bread topped with pineapple jam is a popular teatime accompaniment in Barbados, Antigua, the Bahamas, and Jamaica. "Because of our British heritage," explains Jamaican chef Helen Willinsky, we "still enjoy afternoon tea. Usually we serve toast with guava jelly and a piece of this type of sweet, cake-like bread."[14]

Trifle, a sweet that originated in England but has a tropical flavor on the islands, is another teatime favorite.

Because they are so abundant, tropical fruits influence the sweet treats of the islands.

Caribbean Banana Bread

Banana bread is a popular island snack. It tastes great plain or spread with jam, peanut butter, or cream cheese.

Ingredients
1 cup bananas, mashed
½ cup butter or margarine
1 cup sugar
2 eggs, beaten
1 ½ cups flour
⅔ cup shredded coconut
1 teaspoon baking powder
½ teaspoon baking soda
½ teaspoon vanilla extract

Instructions
1. Preheat the oven to 350 degrees.
2. Mix the butter and sugar until they are creamy. Add the bananas, eggs, and vanilla and mix well.
3. Mix the other ingredients in another bowl. Then add it to the butter mixture. Mix well.
4. Put the mixture into a greased loaf pan. Bake until the loaf is done, about 1 hour. To test, insert a fork or toothpick in the middle of the loaf; when it comes out clean, the loaf is done.
5. Let the loaf cool before slicing and eating.

It consists of layers of cake spread with pineapple or guava jam. The cake is topped with layers of tropical fruit and coconut milk custard. The result is sweet, creamy, and uniquely Caribbean. "This most British of

Banana bread is probably as popular in the islands as it is in the United States.

all desserts," explain the Morgans, "takes an exotic turn when introduced to the flavors of the islands."[15]

Mango fool is another creamy treat. To make it, cooks blend sliced mangos, sugar, and condensed milk together until the whole thing is smooth and creamy. It is then chilled and served like pudding. **Tembleque** (taym-blay-kay), a Puerto Rican coconut treat, is another puddinglike choice. Made with coconut milk, tembleque, which means "quivery" in Spanish, is made in a gelatin mold and trembles like gelatin when it is touched. It even looks like white, opaque gelatin, but it tastes like rich, velvety pudding. Perfumed by coconut and the fresh cinnamon that is sprinkled on top, it also smells heavenly. Experts at Goya Foods Inc., a manufacturer of Caribbean foods, say that it is "a treat for the eyes as well as the tastebuds."[16]

There are also exotic pies such as papaya, coconut, or

Trifle

Trifle is easy to make. You can use any type of cake—yellow, angel food, chocolate, or lemon—any flavor pudding and jam, and any type of fruit, so be creative! Trifle looks pretty if you serve it in a glass bowl.

Ingredients
1 yellow cake
1 package instant vanilla pudding, 3 ounces, prepared and cooled
8 ounces frozen whipped topping, thawed
1 cup strawberry jam
2 bananas, sliced in rounds
1 cup sweetened coconut flakes

Directions
1. Cut the cake into large cubes. Put a layer of cubes on the bottom of a large serving bowl.
2. Spread a layer of jam on the cake, the thickness depending on your taste, then add a layer of sliced bananas. Top with a layer of pudding. Sprinkle with coconut flakes.
3. Add another layer of cake cubes and repeat. Top with whipped topping and coconut.
4. Chill. To serve, scoop out with a spoon.

Serves 6–8.

Delicious trifle can be made with any cake, pudding, or fruit that suits your tastebuds.

Grenadian Nutmeg

Nutmeg ice cream is popular in the islands. About half the world's nutmeg comes from Grenada. The spice, however, did not originate in the Caribbean. It originated in Asia. The English, who once ruled Grenada, as well as many Asian countries, brought it to the island. Today, much of Grenada is covered with nutmeg trees.

Islanders use nutmeg in many ways. The pit of the nutmeg fruit is used to make the popular spice. The stringy flesh that surrounds the pit is made into another spice called mace. The fruit itself is used in jams and jellies.

banana cream. And there are cool and creamy lime pies. In fact, key lime pie, which is so popular in Florida, has its origins in Caribbean lime pie. This light and fluffy pie is pale green in color and tastes both sweet and tart at the same time. The Morgans call it "a tropical classic."[17]

And if snackers prefer something sweeter, there are banana-coconut or mango-chocolate shortcakes. Both are filled with rich cream and topped with colorful fruit. There is also exotic ice cream in flavors like coconut, mango, lime, orange, ginger, and nutmeg.

The choices are mind-boggling. With shops and stands all over the islands offering islanders so many delicious selections, it is no wonder that the Caribbean people love to snack. The wide array of sweet, salty, creamy, crunchy, and spicy treats are hard to resist.

Chapter

4

A Warm Welcome

Caribbean hospitality is famous. Guests are warmly welcomed at Caribbean tables, and everyone, from the closest relatives to new friends, are treated like family. Holidays, especially, are a perfect time to celebrate with others.

Merry Christmas

Christmas is a festive time in the Caribbean. Almost everyone, no matter their religion, celebrates. Sharing food and good times during the Christmas season is a Caribbean tradition. Islanders give each other gifts of food throughout the holiday season. Experts at The Silvertorch, a Web site dedicated to providing

For the festive Christmas dinner, a whole pig is often roasted.

information about life in the Caribbean, explain: "Families prepare food, cakes, and other goodies not only for themselves but for others such as other families, friends, co-workers, fellow church or club members. If, for example, a handyman has to do work in a home at Christmastime, the family for whom he is working might well insist that he sit and be served with at least cake and some homemade drink."[18]

And when it comes to Christmas dinner, family members come from all over to celebrate. It is not uncommon for as many as 50 people to crowd around the holiday table. Although the dishes vary, chances are the main dish will be pork.

Roast pig and baked ham are popular choices.

A Wedding Souvenir

Hospitality at weddings on the Dutch islands of Aruba, Bonaire, and Curaçao extends beyond the wedding celebration. Wedding guests not only enjoy a delicious wedding feast, they are given a gift-wrapped piece of wedding cake to take home as a memento. The cake is known as bolo prieto, which means "black cake."

Bolo prieto is a fruitcake that gets its black color from burnt sugar. The black cake is frosted with creamy snow-white icing and sprinkled with teeny silver candies. It is sweet, rich, and beautiful to look at. Lucky guests get to savor the delectable cake twice, once at the wedding and then again at home.

Roasting a whole baby pig is a custom that early settlers brought to the Caribbean from Spain. In that country, the practice marks festive events. Cooking methods vary. In Cuba, the meat is marinated in **mojo** (moh-ho), a tangy sauce made with garlic, orange, and lime juice. It gives the meat a citrusy scent and flavor. Chunks of lime, orange, grapefruit, garlic, and onions are stuffed inside the pig. Then the pig is wrapped in banana leaves and cooked over a fire pit. Or the whole pig is put on a spit that is hung over the fire. The spit is turned by hand. Usually young family members take turns doing this job. When the meat is done, it is crisp and zesty on the outside and fall-apart tender within. De Mers jokes that eating roast pig at Christmas in the Caribbean is such a treat that "it more than makes up for the absence of snow."[19]

Baked ham with a distinctively Caribbean taste is another Christmas favorite. Island cooks coat the ham with syrup made of brown sugar and water. It gives the ham a sugary glaze. Slices of fresh pineapple are placed on top. As the meat cooks, a rich, sweet, exotic aroma fills the kitchen. The ham's look and taste is even more irresistible. The shiny glaze and the bright yellow fruit rings not only enhance the ham's moist and juicy flavor, but they also make it look like an edible work of art.

The flowers of the sorrel plant are used to make a delicious red drink, called sorrel juice, served at Christmas.

A Dark Red Beverage

Pepperpot or other stews, sweet potato pie, candied yams, pickled onions, rice and peas, fried plantains, plum pudding, and johnnycakes (a type of fried bread) are a just a few of the many dishes that accompany the pork. But no matter what else is on the menu, it is likely that **sorrel** juice, a traditional Christmas drink, will be served too. It is especially popular on the English islands.

Sorrel is a flowering plant that grows wild in the Caribbean. Its red blooms open up right before Christmas. Islanders gather the sweet-scented blossoms and dry them in the sun. They mix the dried blooms with bits of orange peel and locally grown ginger and cloves. Next, they put the fragrant blend in boiling water to steep for at least 24 hours. Then, the liquid is strained and sugar is added.

The drink, which is dark red in color and looks something like cranberry juice, is delicious. It tastes of spices, flowers, sugar, and fruit. Not only that, it is very healthy. It is loaded with vitamins and minerals, as well as **antioxidants**, substances that help strengthen the immune system and fight disease.

For islanders, this healthy drink symbolizes Christmas. "No Christmas is complete without it,"[20] says an expert at Grace Foods, a Caribbean food manufacturer.

Pumpkin Soup

Holiday celebrations continue on New Year's Day, which is also Haitian Independence Day. In the past, Haiti was ruled by France. One of the laws the French rulers made involved pumpkin soup. The soup was considered too fine a dish for Haitian plantation workers. Only members of the French ruling class were permitted to eat it. To show that Haiti had become free, the new government encouraged everyone on the island to eat pumpkin soup on the day that the nation won its independence. Ever since, pumpkin soup has been a traditional way to celebrate New Year's Day throughout the Caribbean, and especially in Haiti, where it is a symbol of freedom. And because New Year's Day is usually a day for visiting, islanders make plenty of this hearty soup. That way everyone who drops by can have a bowlful.

Caribbean pumpkins are different from those that grow in North America. They are neither orange nor round. Caribbean pumpkins are oval, and their skin is green with yellow or white spots. But inside, their flesh is orange. And they have a sweet taste, similar to North American pumpkins.

To make the soup, cooks cut the pumpkin flesh into cubes, which they cook in water or chicken broth with onions, spices, and bits of bacon or salt pork. Other popular ingredients include chili peppers, hot sauce, yams, tomatoes, and beef. The soup is cooked until the pumpkin is soft enough to be mashed with a spoon

Pumpkin soup is a traditional way to celebrate New Year's Day in the Caribbean. To make it even more festive, it is often served from a hollowed-out pumpkin.

Creamy Pumpkin Soup

This soup uses canned pumpkin. Evaporated milk, half-and-half, or coconut milk can be used to make it creamy. You can add or subtract spices and add crumbled bacon or ham chunks, depending on your taste.

Ingredients
16-ounce can pure pumpkin
3 cups chicken broth
1 small onion, chopped
2 tablespoon olive oil
½ teaspoon each of nutmeg, red pepper flakes, and allspice
1 cup evaporated milk

Instructions
1. Heat the oil in a stockpot over medium heat. Add the onion and cook until soft.
2. Add the broth, pumpkin, and spices and bring to a boil over medium heat. Reduce heat to low and simmer for 15 minutes.
3. Put the soup mix in a blender and mix until smooth.
4. Put the soup back in the pot and add the milk. Heat on low to warm the mixture. Do not boil.

Serves 4.

or placed in a blender and pureed until it is smooth as velvet. Then it is put back in the pot and reheated. Some cooks add cream or coconut milk, which makes the soup thick and rich. If the cook really wants to make the dish extra special, the soup is poured into a clean pumpkin shell and served from there.

The soup tastes great hot or cold. No matter the temperature, for many islanders pumpkin soup is as much a part of New Year's Day as hanging up a new calendar. "All Haitians commence the New Year with this soup,"[21] explains Haitian chef, Mirta Yurnet-Thomas.

Fresh Crab for Everyone

Spring brings other celebrations. One of the most fun times occurs on the day after Easter. On this day, groups of islanders gather on the beaches, build fires, and fill cooking pots with freshly caught crabs for all to enjoy.

There are many different varieties of crabs living in the Caribbean, and not all live in water. Ocean crabs are caught in nets and wooden traps, or they may be carefully scooped up as they scuttle across the sand. Once caught, the crabs are killed and their shells are removed. The crabmeat and crab juices are cooked with water, lime juice, chilis, and, often, smoked ham.

Multiaged groups of friends and family sit on beach chairs and blankets or play in the surf and sand just waiting for the crabs to cook. The scent

Carnival in Trinidad

Many Caribbean islanders give up favorite foods during Lent, the 40-day period before Easter. Before Lent begins, people in Trinidad hold a huge outdoor celebration known as Carnival. During Carnival, people crowd the streets. They wear elaborate brightly colored costumes, dance, play steel drums, and eat and drink favorite foods.

During Carnival, food is everywhere. Pelau, a stew of rice, beans, chicken, hot peppers, spices, sugar, and coconut milk is a Carnival favorite. Vendors cook it in huge kettles right on the street. Crab with dumplings and jerk chicken are also popular Carnival fare. There is also ginger beer for adults. It is beer spiced with ginger, which gives the beer an interesting flavor.

Before Lent, Carnival is celebrated in Trinidad with costume, dance, music—and lots of food.

Crab Salad

Cooked crabmeat that is not eaten on the holiday picnic is often turned into delicious crab salad.

Ingredients
1 pound crab meat, cooked, cleaned, and cut in chunks
2 tomatoes, chopped
1 jalapeño pepper, seeds removed and chopped
1 small sweet red onion, chopped
¼ cup lime juice
½ cup green olives, sliced

Instructions
1. Combine all the ingredients in a large bowl. Toss together well.
2. Put the bowl in the refrigerator to marinate for 30 minutes.

Serve with soda crackers.

Any available kind of crab can be used to make this delicious salad.

Islanders celebrate on the day after Easter by catching, cooking, and eating crabs.

of the salt air mixes with that of the sweet and spicy crab stew. "The aroma alone will drive you nuts!"[22] insists Caribbean chef Dorinda Hafner. And the taste—salty, zesty, tart, and sweet all at the same time—is fantastic.

Caribbean islanders love to gather together on holidays and celebrate. Tempting traditional dishes like fresh crab, pumpkin soup, roast pork, and sorrel juice make the occasions more enjoyable and more memorable.

Metric Conversions

Mass (weight)

1 ounce (oz.)	= 28.0 grams (g)
8 ounces	= 227.0 grams
1 pound (lb.) or 16 ounces	= 0.45 kilograms (kg)
2.2 pounds	= 1.0 kilogram

Liquid Volume

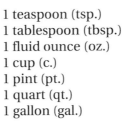

1 teaspoon (tsp.)	= 5.0 milliliters (ml)
1 tablespoon (tbsp.)	= 15.0 milliliters
1 fluid ounce (oz.)	= 30.0 milliliters
1 cup (c.)	= 240 milliliters
1 pint (pt.)	= 480 milliliters
1 quart (qt.)	= 0.96 liters (l)
1 gallon (gal.)	= 3.84 liters

Pan Sizes

8- inch cake pan	= 20 x 4-centimeter cake pan
9-inch cake pan	= 23 x 3.5-centimeter cake pan
11 x 7-inch baking pan	= 28 x 18-centimeter baking pan
13 x 9-inch baking pan	= 32.5 x 23-centimeter baking pan
9 x 5-inch loaf pan	= 23 x 13-centimeter loaf pan
2-quart casserole	= 2-liter casserole

Temperature

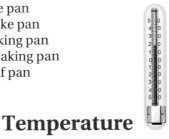

212°F	= 100°C (boiling point of water)
225°F	= 110°C
250°F	= 120°C
275°F	= 135°C
300°F	= 150°C
325°F	= 160°C
350°F	= 180°C
375°F	= 190°C
400°F	= 200°C

Length

1/4 inch (in.)	= 0.6 centimeters (cm)
1/2 inch	= 1.25 centimeters
1 inch	= 2.5 centimeters

Notes

Chapter 1: Exciting and Colorful

1. Jinx Morgan and Jefferson Morgan, *The Sugar Mill Caribbean Cookbook*. Boston: Harvard Common Press, 1996, p. 62.

2. Bruce Geddes, *World Food: Caribbean*. Victoria, Australia: Lonely Planet, p. 39.

3. John De Mers, *Caribbean Cooking*. New York: HP Books, 1997, p. vii.

4. De Mers, *Caribbean Cooking*. p. 16.

5. Steven Raichlen, *The Caribbean Pantry*. New York: Artisan, 1995, p. 57.

6. Raichlen, *The Caribbean Pantry*, p. 8.

Chapter 2: A Bite of History

7. Dorinda Hafner, *A Taste of Africa*. Berkeley, CA: Ten Speed Press, 1993, p. 135.

8. Norman Van Aken, *New World Kitchen*. New York: Harper-Collins, 2003, p. 176.

9. De Mers, *Caribbean Cooking*, p. 143.

Chapter 3: Life Tastes Good

10. Lucretia Bingham, "Calypso, Sequins, and Spice," *Saveur*, March 2006, p. 73.

11. Jessica B. Harris, *Sky Juice and Flying Fish*. New York: Fireside Books, 1991, p. 81.

12. Harris, *Sky Juice and Flying Fish*, p. 89.

13. Van Aken, *New World Kitchen*, p. 13.

14. Helen Willinsky, "Quick Orange Bread," CaribSeek. http://recipes.caribseek.com/Jamaica/quick-orange-bread.shtml.

15. Morgan and Morgan, *The Sugar Mill Caribbean Cookbook*, p. 218.

16. Goya Foods Inc., "Tembleque–Coconut Pudding," www.goya.com/english/recipes/recipe.html?recipeCatID=4&recipeID=77.

17. Morgan and Morgan, *The Sugar Mill Caribbean Cookbook*, p. 210.

Chapter 4: A Warm Welcome
18. The Silvertorch, "Christmas in the Caribbean," www.silvertorch.com/c-christmas.htm.

19. De Mers, *Caribbean Cooking*, p. 132.

20. Grace Foods, "The Best Beverage for Christmas." www.gracefoods.com/site/sorrel-health.

21. Mirta Yurnet-Thomas, "Pumpkin Soup," CaribSeek. www.recipes.caribseek.com/Haiti/pumpkin-soup.shtml.

22. Dorinda Hafner, "Caribbean Antillean Crab Pilaf," Global Destinations. www.globalgourmet.com/destinations/caribbean/crabpilaf.html.

Glossary

ackee: A tropical fruit with yellow pods that taste and look like scrambled eggs when cooked.

antioxidants: Substances that help strengthen the immune system and fight disease.

Arawak Indians: People native to the Caribbean.

blaff: Dish named for the sound the fish makes when it is dropped into the hot poaching liquid.

boucan (boo-can): A cooking method created by the Arawak Indians.

callaloo: Pepperpot soup; also the name for a leafy green vegetable similar to spinach that gives the dish its green color.

canaree: A big pot used by African slaves in the Caribbean.

Carib Indians: People native to the Caribbean.

cassareep (kass-uh-reep): A substance made from the juice of the cassava.

cassava (kas-sah-vuh): A starchy root vegetable.

chicharrones (chee-char-roh-nays): Fried pork rinds.

conch (konk): An edible ocean shellfish with a large spiral shell.

congri: Cuban dish of red beans and rice.

fritters: Fried batter with vegetables, meat, or fish inside.

guavas (gwa-vuhs): Sweet tropical fruits.

jerk pork: A spicy pork dish.

marinated: To flavor food by soaking it in a liquid.

Maroons: The name given to a group of runaway Jamaican slaves.

mojo (moh-ho): A sauce made from garlic, orange, and lime juice.

pepperpot: A spicy stew.

pimento (pee-men-toe): The Caribbean name for allspice.

plantains: A starchy bananalike fruit used in cooking.

poached: Food cooked in a simmering liquid, such as water or broth.

sautéed (saw-tayd): Lightly fried.

sorrel: A flowering plant with red blossoms used to make a Christmas drink.

tembleque (taym-blay-kay): Coconut pudding.

trifle: A layered sweet made with cake, fruit, and cream.

For Further Exploration

Books

Alison Behnke, *Cooking the Cuban Way*. Minneapolis: Lerner Books, 2004. A Cuban cookbook for kids.

Cheryl Davidson Kaufman, *Cooking the Caribbean Way*. Minneapolis: Lerner Books, 2002. A Caribbean cookbook for kids.

Julie McCulloch, *The Caribbean*. Chicago: Heineman, 2001. A simple Caribbean cookbook for kids.

Anne Wallace Sharp, *Indigenous People of the World: The Caribbean*. San Diego: Lucent Books, 2003. Discusses the different Indian groups who lived in the Caribbean.

Web Sites

Caribbean Choice (www.caribbeanchoice.com/main.asp). A Web site dedicated to Caribbean travel. It has pictures and videos of every island, recipes, news, and a market selling Caribbean items.

CaribSeek (www.caribseek.com). Offers lots of information about the different nations of the Caribbean, including recipes, photos, maps, and coats of arms, as well as offering Caribbean foods and gift items for sale.

Sheppard Software, "All About the Caribbean," (www.sheppardsoftware.com/Caribbean_Geography. htm). Lots of information, maps, and games about the different Caribbean nations just for kids.

United States Dept. of Agriculture, National Forest Service, "Caribbean National Forest," (www.fs.fed. us/r8/caribbean/kids-page/index.shtml). Information about the animals and plants that live in the rain forest in Puerto Rico.

Index

Ackee, 12, 14
Afternoon tea, 37–39
Allspice, 16
Antioxidants, 47
Arawak Indians, 6, 14, 20–21, 26
Aruba, 4, 45
Asians, 31

Bahamas, 4, 32
Baked ham, 44, 46
Banana coconut bread, 38, 39, 40
Barbados, 8
Beans, 31–32
Black-eyed peas, 31
Blaff, 8
Bolo prieto, 45
Bonaire, 45
Boucan, 21
British influences, 37–39, 42
Buccaneers, 21

Callaloo, 26
Canaree, 25
Carib Indians, 6
Caribbean, 4
Caribbean banana bread (recipe), 39
Carnival, 52
Cashew nuts, 9
Cassareep, 26
Cassava, 26, 28
Chicharrones, 33, 34
Chicken, jerk, 23–24

Chickens, 22–23
Chili peppers, 16, 18–19
Christmas, 43–47
Cinnamon, 16
Climate, 4, 20
Coconut milk, 13, 40
Coconuts, 13, 38
Conch, 7, 8
Conch fritters, 35–36
Congri, 31
Coo-coo, 8
Cooking techniques, 7–8, 20–22
Crab salad (recipe), 53
Crabs, 7, 51, 54
Cuba, 4, 31
Curaçao, 45
Curry dishes, 21

De Mers, John, 10, 12, 32, 45–46
Djon djon, 31
Dominican Republic, 4

Easter, 51
European settlers, 31, 36, 37, 45

Fish, 4, 6–10
Fish fritters, 35–36
Fishing, 7
Flying fish, 7, 8
Food regions, 5
Foreign influences, 21–23, 31, 36, 37, 42, 45

France, 37
Fried snacks, 33–37
Fritters, 33–36
Fruit salad (recipe), 15
Fruits
  candied, 37
  tropical, 4, 10–14

Geddes, Bruce, 8
Ginger beer, 52
Glacés, 37
Goya Foods, 40
Grenada, 16, 28, 42
Guadeloupe, 31, 37
Guavas, 14

Hafner, Dorinda, 23, 54
Haiti, 4, 31, 37, 48
Ham, baked, 44, 46
Harris, Jessica B., 34
Herbs, 14, 16–17
Holidays
  Carnival, 52
  Christmas, 43–47
  Easter, 51
  New Year's Day, 48, 49, 51
Hospitality, 43, 45
Hot peppers, 16, 18–19
Hot sauces, 16, 17, 18–19

Ice cream, 42
India, 21

Jamaica, 4, 21–23, 32

Jerk dishes, 21–25
Jerk huts, 23
Jerky, 25

Key lime pie, 40, 42
Kidney beans, 32

Lent, 52
Lima beans, 31
Lime pies, 40, 42
Lobster, 7

Mango fool, 40
Mangos, 14
Marinades, 8, 20–25, 45
Markets, 11
Maroons, 21–22
Martinique, 31, 37
Meat
  marinades for, 20–25
  preservation of, 20,
    22, 25
Mofongo, 10, 14
Mojo, 45
Moors and Christians,
  31
Morgan, Jefferson, 7, 42
Morgan, Jinx, 7, 42
Mortar and pestle, 10

New Year's Day, 48,
  49, 51
Nutmeg, 42
Nuts, 9

One-pot meals, 25–29
Orange bread, 38
Outdoor markets, 11

Papayas, 12, 14, 35

Peas, 29–32
Pepperpot, 26, 28–29
Peppers, hot, 16, 18–19
Pies, 40, 42
Pig, roast, 44–46
Pigeon peas, 31–32
Pigs, 22–23
Pimento, 16
Pirates, 21
Plantain chips, 33, 34
Plantains, 14
Poached fish, 8
Pork
  chicharrones, 34
  jerk, 21–22
Puerto Rico, 4, 31
Pumpkin soup, 48–51

Raichlen, Steven, 18, 19
Recipes
  Caribbean banana
    bread, 39
  crab salad, 53
  fruit salad, 15
  hot and spicy nuts, 9
  jerk chicken, 24
  pumpkin soup, 50
  ropa vieja, 27
  trifle, 41
Red snapper, 7
Rice, 29–32
Roast pig, 44–46
Ropa vieja, 27
Roti, 21

Saltfish, 36
Sautéed fish, 8
Scotch bonnet, 18
Seafood, 4, 6–10, 35–37
Shark, 7

Shark and bake, 36
Shortcakes, 42
Shrimp, 7
Silvertorch, 43–44
Sky juice, 14
Slaves, 21–22, 25, 28–
  29, 31
Snacks
  fried, 33–37
  seafood, 35–37
  sweet, 37–42
Sopa de quingombo, 26
Sorrel juice, 46, 47
Soup, pumpkin, 48–51
Spanish settlers, 31, 45
Spices, 4, 14, 16–17, 23
Stamp and go, 35–36
Sugar, 37
Sweet treats, 37–42
Swordfish, 7

Teatime, 37–39
Tembleque, 40
Thyme, 16
Trifle, 38–39, 41
Trinidad, 21, 33, 52
Tropical fruits, 4, 10–
  14, 38

U.S. Virgin Islands, 10,
  31–32

Van Aken, Norman,
  29, 36
Virgin Islands, 10,
  31–32

Weddings, 45
Willinsky, Helen, 38

About the Author

Barbara Sheen is the author of numerous works of fiction and nonfiction for young people, including more than a dozen books in the A Taste of Culture series. She lives in New Mexico with her family. In her spare time, she likes to swim, walk, garden, and read. Of course, she loves to cook!